ELI MANNING

BY ALEX MONNIG

Published by ABDO Publishing Company, PO Box 398166, Minneapolis, MN 55439. Copyright © 2013 by Abdo Consulting Group, Inc. International copyrights reserved in all countries. No part of this book may be reproduced in any form without written permission from the publisher. SportsZone™ is a trademark and logo of ABDO Publishing Company.

Printed in the United States of America,
North Mankato, Minnesota
052012
092012

 THIS BOOK CONTAINS AT LEAST 10% RECYCLED MATERIALS.

Editor: Chrös McDougall
Series Designer: Craig Hinton

Photo Credits: Greg Trott/AP Images, cover, 1; Paul Spinelli/AP Images, 4; Elaine Thompson/AP Images, 7; Sporting News/Getty Images, 8; David Rae Morris/AP Images, 10; Lubbock Avalanche-Journal, Jim Watkins/AP Images, 13; Tim Sharp/AP Images, 15; John Marshall Mantel/AP Images, 16; Bill Kostroun/AP Images, 19; David Drapkin/AP Images, 21; Tom Hauck/AP Images, 22; Paul Hiffmeyer/Disneyland/AP Images, 24; Sharon Ellman/AP Images, 27; Perry Knotts/AP Images, 29

Library of Congress Cataloging-in-Publication Data
Monnig, Alex.
  Eli Manning : super bowl hero / Alex Monnig.
    p. cm. -- (Playmakers)
  Includes index.
  ISBN 978-1-61783-549-0
  1. Manning, Eli, 1981---Juvenile literature. 2. Football players--United States--Biography--Juvenile literature. 3. Quarterbacks (Football)--United States--Biography--Juvenile literature. I. Title.
  GV939.M2887M66 2012
  796.332092--dc23
  [B]
                                    2012015022

TABLE OF CONTENTS

Eli Manning

CHAPTER 1

A GIANT UPSET

Eli Manning and the New York Giants were running out of time. It was Super Bowl XLII. It was late in the fourth quarter. And the New England Patriots held a 14–10 lead.

The Patriots were dominant during that 2007–08 season. They had won all 16 regular-season games plus two playoff games. Most experts thought they would win the Super Bowl. No team had ever finished 19–0. But Eli and the Giants had hung around.

New York Giants quarterback Eli Manning looks for a receiver during Super Bowl XLII.

There was just 1:15 left in the game. And the Giants still had a shot to win. New York had the ball on its own 44-yard line.

Eli was New York's quarterback. He took the snap and looked for receivers. But he could not find any. New England defenders closed in on Eli. They nearly sacked him. But Eli stayed on his feet. He scrambled away. Finally he fired the ball down the field.

The pass was high. But it was close to Giants wide receiver David Tyree. And Tyree jumped as high as he could. He was able to trap the ball against his helmet. Tyree fell to the ground. But somehow he hung on to it. It was good for a 32-yard gain. The Giants were within striking distance.

Four plays later, they struck. Wide receiver Plaxico Burress was open in the end zone. Eli passed to him for a touchdown. The Giants added the extra point. That gave them a 17–14 lead.

Eli had solid numbers in Super Bowl XLII. They were not eye-popping numbers, though. He threw for 255 yards, two touchdowns, and one interception. But that was enough to earn him the Most Valuable Player (MVP) Award for the game.

The New York Giants' David Tyree traps the football against his helmet for a famous catch late in Super Bowl XLII.

Less than a minute remained. The Giants' defense held strong. New York won the game. It was one of the biggest upsets in Super Bowl history. And it was also Eli's first Super Bowl win. But it was not the first Super Bowl in the Manning family.

Eli is part of a famous football family. It began with his father, Archie Manning. Archie was a star quarterback in college at Mississippi from 1968 to 1970. The school is also known as

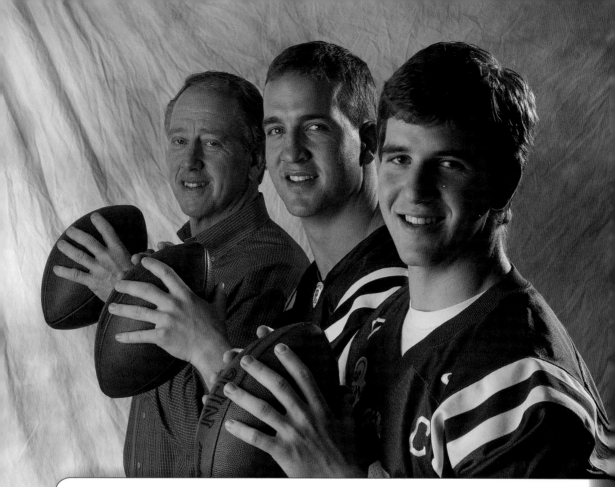

Archie Manning, *left*, Peyton Manning, *center*, and Eli Manning were all star quarterbacks in high school, college, and the NFL.

Ole Miss. He was later voted into the College Football Hall of Fame. Archie starred in the National Football League (NFL) after that. He played mostly for the New Orleans Saints.

Archie and Olivia Manning had three sons. Elisha "Eli" Nelson Manning was the youngest. He was born on

January 3, 1981, in New Orleans, Louisiana. The Manning kids grew up in New Orleans. Football was a way of life for them. But Archie never forced his children to play. All three loved the sport just like their dad. And all three became football stars.

Eli's oldest brother is Cooper Manning. Cooper was a star wide receiver in high school. Many expected him to star in college too. But a medical condition ended his playing days early. Eli's other brother is Peyton Manning. Some consider Peyton to be one of the best quarterbacks ever. He starred for the Tennessee Volunteers in college. Then he shined in the NFL. He played 13 seasons with the Indianapolis Colts. He led them to the Super Bowl twice. The Colts won Super Bowl XLI in 2007. Peyton signed with the Denver Broncos in 2012.

All three brothers played for the team at Isidore Newman High School. Peyton was a natural leader. Eli was quiet and had to grow into that role. The school's starting quarterback was suspended one game during Eli's freshman year. So Eli started in his place and shined. Eli was still pretty shy. But his coach knew then that Eli could be a team leader.

Eli Manning

CHAPTER 2

OLE ELI AND THE REBELS

Eli Manning took over as Isidore Newman High School's starting quarterback as a sophomore. Many people remembered Peyton Manning's success there. That put some pressure on Eli. But he largely lived up to the hype. He threw for more than 7,421 yards in high school. He also threw for 81 touchdowns. Eli's best year was his last. He led Isidore Newman to the state quarterfinals.

Manning surveys the field during a 1997 game while playing quarterback for Isidore Newman High School.

Peyton Manning had been a loud and fiery leader in high school. But Eli Manning was more laid back. That is why Isidore Newman coach Frank Gendusa nicknamed him "Easy."

Many college football coaches wanted Manning to choose their school. Football is a big deal in the South. The fans are very passionate about their teams. So fans at Ole Miss were thrilled when Manning decided to go there. After all, Archie Manning had been one of the Rebels' all-time greats.

The fans would have to wait to see the youngest Manning. The coaches decided to redshirt him his first year. That meant he could not play in games that year. But he could still practice with the team. He would also still have four years to play in games.

Manning got into some trouble after that year. He was arrested for public drunkenness. He was also underage. That arrest embarrassed Manning. He never wanted that to happen again. So he focused more on school and football after that.

Manning still did not play much in his second year. However, he took over the starting role in his third year, in 2001.

After a redshirt season and one as a backup, Manning took over as the starting quarterback at Ole Miss in 2001.

And he quickly made his mark. Some great Ole Miss players had left after the 2000 season. But the team hardly missed a beat behind Manning. The Rebels averaged 35.5 points per game in 2001. That was tenth highest average in the country.

Now Manning was known as a top college quarterback. But he had a tough task ahead of him. The Southeastern

The Heisman Trophy is awarded to the best college football player each season. Both Peyton and Archie Manning had fallen just shy of winning the trophy. Eli Manning was a front-runner for the award as a senior. But he fell just short too. Manning finished third in the voting. Oklahoma quarterback Jason White won the award.

Conference (SEC) had many strong teams. Most believed other teams were more talented than Ole Miss. That put a lot of pressure on Manning. He and his team struggled a bit in 2002. The Rebels lost five games in a row at one point. Manning threw 10 interceptions during that stretch. But he did not let those struggles define him. Manning still finished with good passing numbers.

Players can go to the NFL Draft after three college seasons. Some people thought Manning would do that. But he really wanted to bring success to Ole Miss. So he came back. The Rebels began the season 2–2. That ended their hopes for a national championship. But Manning was known for his ability to stay calm. He led the Rebels to wins in eight of their final nine games. The only loss came against Louisiana State University. That team went on to win the national title.

Manning prepares to throw the ball during the 2004 Cotton Bowl against Oklahoma State.

Manning fell short of leading Ole Miss to an SEC title and a national championship. But he did help the Rebels become a major player nationally. He also earned his college degree in marketing. Manning worked hard in school. The SEC named him to its academic honor roll in 2000, 2001, and 2002.

Manning had proven to be a top college quarterback. It was clear that his next stop was the NFL. And most expected a team to choose him early in the 2004 NFL Draft.

Eli Manning

CHAPTER 3

A ROUGH START

The San Diego Chargers had the first pick in the 2004 NFL Draft. Many thought they would select Eli Manning. But Manning told the team he did not want to play there.

The Chargers picked Manning anyway. He appeared unhappy when the pick was announced. But Manning was not a member of the Chargers for long. The New York Giants had the fourth pick. They selected quarterback Philip Rivers. He had been a star

Manning holds up a San Diego Chargers jersey after the team selected him first in the 2004 NFL Draft.

at North Carolina State. Then the Giants and Chargers swapped quarterbacks about one hour later. They also traded other draft picks to make it more even.

Manning had gotten his wish. But he had upset some people along the way. Fans did not like that he had been picky about where he would play. Manning faced a lot of pressure to succeed after that. He also faced a lot of pressure just by being in New York City. It is the biggest city in the United States. And the media there can be very harsh.

The media had plenty to complain about in Manning's rookie year. Kurt Warner started at quarterback for the Giants. But they stumbled to a 5–4 start. So coach Tom Coughlin named Manning his starter. Coughlin hoped Manning could bring fresh life to the team. But NFL players are much faster and

Eli and Peyton Manning do not always enjoy playing against each other. But there is often a lot of excitement among fans when they do. The brothers first faced off in the 2006 season opener. Peyton's Colts won 26–21. They also played in 2010. The Colts again won, this time 38–14.

Manning looks for an open receiver during his first NFL start, a 14–10 loss to the Atlanta Falcons in 2004.

stronger than college players. Rookie quarterbacks often need time to adjust. That was the case with Manning. His fourth game as starter was his worst. Manning was 4-for-18 passing. He threw for just 27 yards and two interceptions. Finally, Coughlin put Warner back in.

Manning was back starting the next week. But the results were the same. The Giants ended the season a disappointing

6–10. Some fans were frustrated. But the New York players respected Manning. They liked how he handled the hard season. Coughlin was a demanding coach. He pushed Manning hard. But he believed in his young quarterback, too. That started paying off in 2005.

Manning was the starter from the first day of practice. That showed him that the team had confidence in him. And Manning quickly showed how much he had learned. His 3,762 passing yards were the fifth most in the NFL that season. And his 24 touchdowns were the fourth most. But he once again had trouble with interceptions. Only one quarterback had more than Manning's 17 interceptions.

New York made the playoffs with an 11–5 record. But Manning struggled against the Carolina Panthers in the first round. He threw three interceptions in the 23–0 loss.

It was hard at times during Manning's early years. He was often in the spotlight playing in New York. Fans wanted him to match his brother's success. Peyton Manning was shredding defenses for the Indianapolis Colts. And some football fans also still held a grudge against Eli after the 2004 draft.

Manning struggled in his first playoff appearance, in 2006. The Giants lost 23–0 to the Carolina Panthers.

The pressure really started to build during the 2006 season. Manning played very well at times. But both he and the Giants struggled at times too. Fans and even some teammates began to question Manning's leadership abilities. They saw Peyton confidently barking orders to his teammates at the line. Then they compared that to the quieter Eli and his struggling Giants.

Manning holds the Lombardi Trophy after leading the New York Giants to victory over the New England Patriots in Super Bowl XLII.

New York finished the regular season at just 8–8. But that was still good enough for a return trip to the playoffs. However, the Giants again lost in the first round. This time, the Philadelphia Eagles beat them 23–20.

A lot was riding on Manning's 2007 season. Fans knew he was a good quarterback. But they wanted to see if he could truly be a great quarterback.

Manning was selected for his first Pro Bowl in 2008. That is an exhibition game for all the best players in the NFL each season. He also made the Pro Bowl in 2011.

The answer appeared to be no. Manning's 20 interceptions were the most in the NFL.

Manning still put up good numbers otherwise. And the Giants finished 10–6. That meant they got to go back to the playoffs. And this time, they got hot. The Giants beat the Tampa Bay Buccaneers, the Dallas Cowboys, and the Green Bay Packers. Manning threw four touchdowns and zero interceptions in those wins.

That set up the Super Bowl XLII showdown with the New England Patriots. New England was heavily favored. But when that game was over, the Giants were champions. Manning also had quieted his critics—at least for now.

CHAPTER 4

SUPER MANNING

New York Giants fans believed they finally had an elite quarterback in Eli Manning. And he continued to improve. Manning cut down on his turnovers in 2008. The Giants finished 12–4 and headed to the playoffs. But the Philadelphia Eagles beat them 23–11 in the first round.

Manning still had reason to smile in 2008. He married Abby McGrew on April 19 in San José del Cabo, Mexico. They had met in college. Eli and Abby

Manning and his new wife Abby ride the Astro Orbitor at California's Disneyland in May 2008.

had their first child three years later. Ava Frances Manning was born in March 2011.

But life on the football field soon turned sour. The Giants had made the playoffs for four straight seasons. Then the team missed the playoffs in 2009 and 2010. Manning showed flashes of greatness. But fans were frustrated when he led the league with 25 interceptions in 2010.

Things did not look much better when the Giants started 7–7 in 2011. It appeared they would again fall short of the playoffs. But Manning was working hard to be a better leader. And he helped the Giants win their final two games and make the playoffs.

The Green Bay Packers were heavily favored to win the Super Bowl. Their only loss was late in the season with little on

Manning told reporters before the 2011 season that he believed he was an elite quarterback. The reactions were mixed. Fans argued about whether he truly was one of the best. But Giants fans were excited to hear Manning's confidence. They were even more excited when he backed up his words in Super Bowl XLVI.

Manning prepares to hand the ball off against the Dallas Cowboys during a 2011 game.

the line. Fans wondered if any team could beat the Packers in the playoffs.

Then the Giants rolled past the Atlanta Falcons in the first round. People began to sense that maybe the Giants could beat the Packers. And that is what they did in the second round.

Manning threw for 330 yards, three touchdowns, and one interception in that game. New York easily won by a score of 37–20. Like in 2008, the Giants were getting hot at just the right time. Then they beat the favored San Francisco 49ers in overtime on the road. That sent the Giants back to the Super Bowl.

The Giants again faced the New England Patriots in Super Bowl XLVI. And once again, most people favored the Patriots. They saw it as a chance for New England to make up for the heartbreaking loss in 2008.

New England appeared on its way to getting that revenge. The Patriots led 17–15 with 3:46 left in the game. But that is when the Giants got the ball back. They started the drive at their 12-yard line. Manning thrived in those types of situations. He had led six game-winning, fourth-quarter drives that season. Now he went to work on another one.

The first play quickly became an all-time Super Bowl highlight. Manning fired a perfect 38-yard throw to wide receiver Mario Manningham. The ball barely made it between two Patriots defenders. Manningham was able to grab it as he fell out of bounds. The Giants were on a roll after that. And eight plays later they scored a touchdown to take a 21–17 lead.

The Giants' defense held on for the final 57 seconds. And just like that, Manning and the Giants had won another Super

Manning celebrates after leading the Giants to victory over the New England Patriots in Super Bowl XLVI.

Bowl. Manning again was named the MVP. He threw for 296 yards with a touchdown. More importantly, he did not throw an interception.

Winning one Super Bowl is hard enough. Even Peyton Manning had only won a single Super Bowl through the 2012 game. After winning two titles, Eli Manning finally proved his status as an elite quarterback.

FUN FACTS AND QUOTES

- By winning Super Bowl XLII, Eli Manning and the New York Giants kept the New England Patriots from having a perfect 19–0 season. But the Giants almost stopped New England's undefeated season earlier than that. In the last game of the regular season, New York lost to New England by just three points, 38–35.

- Growing up, Eli's older brothers Cooper and Peyton often watched footage of their father Archie. They asked Archie what it was like being a quarterback in the NFL. But Eli kept his love of football more to himself. He did not show much interest in his father's playing days.

- Manning has proven to be a tough and reliable quarterback over the years. Since being named the starter in 2004 through the 2011 season, he has started every single game for the Giants. Manning has played through some injuries during that time.

- During the off-season, the Mannings live in Oxford, Mississippi. That is where Ole Miss is located.

WEB LINKS

To learn more about Eli Manning, visit ABDO Publishing Company online at **www.abdopublishing.com**. Websites about Manning are featured on our Book Links page. These links are routinely monitored and updated to provide the most current information available.

GLOSSARY

conference
In sports, a group of teams that plays each other each season.

critics
People who judge how well or how poorly a player plays.

draft
A system used by professional sports leagues to select new players in order to spread incoming talent among all teams. The NFL Draft is held each spring.

drive
A series of offensive plays.

exhibition
A game that does not count for competitive advantage. Exhibitions are often meant for the fans' enjoyment.

interception
A pass thrown by a quarterback that is caught by a member of the opposing defense.

media
Organizations that provide information to the public, such as newspapers and magazines, radio and television, and the Internet.

overtime
An extra session of football played when a game is tied after four regulation periods.

redshirt
A year in which a college athlete practices with a team but does not play in games and therefore does not lose a year of eligibility.

rookie
A first-year player in the NFL.

upset
A result where the supposedly worse team defeats the supposedly better team.

INDEX

FURTHER RESOURCES

Gitlin, Marty. *New York Giants.* Edina, MN: ABDO Publishing Co., 2010.

Maxymuk, John. *Game Changers: The Greatest Plays in New York Giants History.* Chicago: Triumph Books, 2010.

Vacchiano, Ralph. *Eli Manning: The Making of a Quarterback.* New York: Skyhorse Publishing, 2008.